The Dead Sound in Siren

When We Hear The Sound We Drift

A Siren Documentary

Elizabeth J Whitaker

Table of contents

Chapter 1

Origin

The Sirens are perhaps the most fascinating animal in Greek folklore and western culture. Known for their hauntingly delightful singing, the Sirens would bait mariners near perilous rocks and wrecks. Their presence in current times contrasts immensely with the portrayals and legends of the alarms in Ancient Greece. Here is a more critical glance at it.

Who are the Sirens?
The beginning of the Sirens is in all likelihood Asian. They might have turned into a piece of Greek folklore through the

impact of Asian practices in craftsman ships of Ancient Greece. Contingent upon the creator, the parentage of the Sirens changes, however, most sources concur that they

were the little girls of the waterway god Achelous with one of the Muses.

Early portrayals of the Sirens showed them as half-lady half-bird animals, like nags, who lived by the ocean. In any case, later on, Sirens were said to have female heads and middles, with fishtails from their navel downwards. Around the Middle Ages, the Sirens transformed into the figure that we currently call mermaids.
In Homer's Odyssey, there were just two alarms. Different creators allude to no less than three.

The Sirens Greek folklore

As per a few sources, the Sirens were ladies who were the mates or the workers of Persephone. After this point, the fantasies fluctuate on how they transformed into the hazardous animals they turned out to be.

A few stories suggest that Demeter rebuffed the Sirens for not having the option to

safeguard Persephone when Hades assaulted her. Different sources, notwithstanding, say that they were enthusiastically searching for Persephone and requested that Demeter give them wings so they could fly over the oceans in their hunt.

The Sirens remained on an island close to the waterway of Scylla and Charybdis after the quest for Persephone finished. From that point, they would go after the boats passing close by, alluring the mariners with their beguiling singing. Their singing was wonderful to the point that they could make the breeze stop to pay attention to them. It's from these singing animals that we get the English word alarm, and that implies a gadget that makes an admonition commotion.

With their melodic capacity, they pulled in the mariners from the passing boats, who might come increasingly close to the

perilous rough shore of the Sirens' island and at last gct wrecked and run on the rocks. As per a few legends, the cadavers of their casualties could be tracked down up and down the shores of their island.
The Sirens versus The Muses

So extraordinary was their gift for singing that the Sirens took part in a challenge with the Muses, the goddesses of expressions and motivation. In the fantasies, Hera persuaded the Sirens to go up against the Muses with their singing. The Muses won the challenge and culled out the quills of the Sirens to make themselves crowns.

The Sirens and Odysseus

In Odysseus' long and meandering excursion home from the Trojan War, he needed to go past the island of the Sirens. The sorcerer Circe made sense of the legend of how the singing of the Sirens functioned and how they utilized it to kill the mariners who cruised by. Odysseus

trained his man to hinder their ears with wax so they wouldn't pay attention to the singing. Be that as it may, Odysseus was interested to hear what the singing seemed like. In this way, he chose to attach himself to the pole of the boat so he could pay attention to the singing of the alarms without risk. Like that, Odysseus and his men could cruise by their island and proceed with their excursion.

The Sirens versus Orpheus

The alarms likewise assume a minor part in the fantasies of the incomparable Greek legend Jason and the Argonauts. The cruising team needed to pass close to the island of the Sirens, and they required a method for doing it without being hurt by them. Dissimilar to Odysseus, they didn't utilize wax, however, they had the great legend Orpheus sing and played the lyre while cruising by the island. The melodic abilities of Orpheus were unbelievable, and they were sufficient to make different

mariners center around his singing instead of on the singing of the Sirens. Accordingly, the Sirens were no counterpart for the singing of Orpheus, the renowned performer.

The Death of the Sirens
There was a prescience that said that the Sirens would pass on assuming that a human was ever to oppose their tempting procedures. Since both Orpheus and

Odysseus figured out how to endure their experience, it is hazy which of them caused the passing of the Sirens. One way or another, after they neglected to draw in the humans, the Sirens hurled themselves entirely into the sea and serious self-destruction.

Sirens versus Mermaids
These days, there is disarray about what alarms are. In the first fantasies, the Sirens were like the wenches, a blend of lady and a bird. They were dull and wound animals

who pulled in mariners with their gift for singing just to kill them. Notwithstanding, their later portrayals show them as lovely fish ladies, whose sexuality attracted men to their demise.
Mermaids are accepted to have started in Assyria yet can be tracked down in many societies, from Japanese to German legends. These animals were portrayed as lovely ladies, normally harmony cherishing, who

attempted to avoid people. Singing was not one of their properties.

Sooner or later ever, the fantasies of the two animals ran into each other, and their attributes became blended. This misguided judgment has impacted the abstract works as well. A few interpretations of Homer's Odyssey allude to the alarms of the first composition as mermaids, giving a misleading thought of the animals Odysseus experienced on his return.

Today, the terms alarm and mermaid are equivalents. Notwithstanding, the term alarm conveys a more regrettable underlying meaning than a mermaid, due to their relationship with death and obliteration.
Imagery of Sirens
The Sirens represent enticement and want, which can prompt obliteration and chance.

On the off chance that a human stopped to pay attention to the lovely hints of the Sirens, they wouldn't have the option to control their cravings and this would lead them to their demise. Accordingly, the Sirens can likewise be said to address sin.

Some have proposed that the Sirens address the base power that females have over men, which can both intrigue and scare men.

After Christianity started to spread, the image of the Sirens was utilized to depict the risks of allurement.

The expression alarm melody is utilized to portray something engaging and appealing yet additionally possibly risky and unsafe.

Sirens in Modern Culture
In current times, the possibility of the Sirens as mermaids has generally spread. They

show up in different films, books, and works of art. By the way, a couple of these portrayals show them as the first Sirens from the fantasies. We could say that the greater part of them are depictions of mermaids, all things considered. Most portrayals of half-lady half-bird animals allude to the Harpies, not to the Sirens. In this sense, the first alarms from Greek folklore have been left to the side.

Sirens imagery
In short
The Sirens were noteworthy characters in two well-known misfortunes from Ancient Greece. The narratives of both Odysseus and the Argonauts incorporate portrayals of the

Sirens and show them as they were in Greek folklore. They are one of the most well-known Greek legendary animals.

END-OF-LIFE CONCERNS
Final breath When Someone Is Dying

Being Present

What is the final breath? Assuming that you are focusing on a friend or family member somewhat recently in life, you might be vexed in the wake of catching wind of the final breath that may one day come. Or on the other hand, you might hear disturbing breath sounds now and keep thinking about whether this is the end.

We should discuss what the final breath implies. This article makes sense of what the final breath means for friends and family, why the perishing individual isn't terrified by it, and things you can do to attempt to improve it.

What Death Rattle Means

The "final breath" is a sort of murmuring sound that you might hear when individuals are kicking the bucket. It happens because they are as of now not ready to swallow or hack, so spit develops toward the rear of the throat and upper aviation routes. The liquid causes the shaking sound when air goes through.

It gives off an impression of being somewhat more normal in ladies yet in any case can show up in individuals of all ages who are passing on for any reason. The "final breath" happens somewhat in generally 50% of individuals who are dying.1

Individuals have needed to find out about death and kicking the bucket, and science has shown that it's a functioning cycle. There are steps in how the body closes down, similarly as there were ventures upon entering the world, during the youngster years, and in different phases of life. The final breath is one of those means and it

probably implies that passing is exceptionally close.

Is It Uncomfortable?

The final breath can be extremely hard so that relatives can hear. In any case, a typical finish-of-life-altering situation isn't awkward for the people who are biting the dust, regardless of whether the individual appears to be to some extent conscious. It doesn't imply that the individual is "suffocating" or having a "terrible" death.2

Individuals who have a final breath while passing on experience no more difficulty breathing than the people who don't have one. Moreover, the nature of the final breath sounds you hear — how noisy they are, for instance — isn't a proportion of how much breathing trouble there is. Indeed, even a portion of the medicines for a final breath will not be guaranteed to change the sounds.

Final breath sounds can be uproarious, however, they are not disturbing to the individual who is kicking the bucket.

As opposed to the withering individual, be that as it may, the final breath can be extremely disturbing for friends and family, and guardians. In one review, no less than 66% of friends and family of an individual biting the dust found that standing by listening to thc final breath is profoundly distressing.2

There are ways of evaporating a portion of the overabundant liquid that causes a final breath, however, recollecting that it is a normal move toward the perishing system. Your adored one doesn't feel like they are suffocating because they are breathing along these lines.

Is There a Treatment?

On the off chance that the final breath is making you restless, there are a couple of things you can attempt. They include:

Prescriptions for liquid development: If you have a hospice solace unit, it probably has a drug for evaporating the liquids. This is normally either atropine or scopolamine.3 Changing your cherished one's situation: The final breath might appear to be more regrettable when somebody is lying level on their back.

Just turning your cherished ones over a piece might help. You can likewise take a stab at setting the head higher than the body and going it aside to assist the liquids with depleting.
How Near Is Death?
Many individuals can't help thinking about how long it will be til' the very end when somebody fosters a final breath. It differs a great deal from one individual to another and makes it hard to foresee precisely the

exact thing the clatter implies concerning time.

You might think about what else to anticipate in the last phases of death. Terminal fretfulness is normal right now, and your cherished one might show up extremely unsettled.

They additionally may communicate close passing mindfulness and let you know they are biting the dust. Many individuals as of now discuss seeing friends and family who have kicked the bucket previously, and certain individuals even start to grin. Try not to attempt to address your adored one, simply love them.

Normal Symptoms toward the End of Life
Being Present
Being with your cherished one while they are biting the dust is testing, yet it is

extremely adoring. At the point when individuals discuss their biggest trepidation

throughout everyday life, usually, they will bite the dust alone. Your presence is the best gift you can at any point give.

Try not to quit conversing with your adored one. Though hearing is the last sense to vanish, and regardless of whether they seem oblivious, they might in any case detect your presence or hear what you are talking about. Simultaneously, you want to deal with yourself as your cherished one would wish. Everybody needs a break sometimes, and this is a higher priority than at any other time. The fact that time is short makes the last breath only one sign. Don't hesitate for even a moment to take a second to stride away on the off chance that you want to.

The "final breath" is one sign that the end is very close, maybe surprisingly fast. It is extremely normal when somebody kicks the bucket. The sputtering sound is brought about by liquid that your cherished one can never again hack up or swallow. It is difficult to hear, however, it is great to realize that it doesn't do any harm or mischief to your cherished one.

Some of the time realizing a thing doesn't make it any more straightforward to encounter. That might be valid as you stand by listening to a friend or family member with a final breath, knowing in your mind that it's a typical piece of the perishing system yet feeling the misery in your heart. That is normal as well. Make it a point to talk it over with a relative, the hospice group, or another person you trust to discuss these thoughts with.

Is murmuring equivalent to a final breath?

Murmuring most frequently depicts the sound of liquid in the lungs. It can happen as a component of the demise cycle. "Final breath" normally alludes to the commotion of spit pooling toward the rear of the throat.

Instructions to Identify and Treat Death Rattle/Wet Respirations

How might you tell a friend or family member is close to death?

Cold skin, loud breathing, and loss of cognizance are among the signs that demise might be close. Not every person will display every one of them, yet it's great to realize them so you're ready to help your adored one without showing dread or alert.

What Befalls the Body at the Time of Death?

How long will an individual life once they foster a final breath?

Commonly, a final breath will start when an individual is hours from passing on, albeit certain individuals might keep on living for a little while.

Chapter 2

END-OF-LIFE CONCERNS

What is the final breath? Assuming that you are focusing on a friend or family member somewhat recently in life, you might be disturbed in the wake of catching wind of the final breath that may one day come. Or on the other hand, you might hear disturbing breath sounds now and keep thinking about whether this is the end.

We should discuss what the final breath implies. This article makes sense of what the final breath means for friends and family, why the perishing individual isn't terrified by it, and things you can do to attempt to improve it.

What Death Rattle Means
The "final breath" is a sort of sputtering sound that you might hear when individuals are passing on. It happens because they are at this point not ready to swallow or hack, so spit develops toward the rear of the throat and upper aviation routes. The liquid causes the shaking sound when air goes through.

It has all the earmarks of being somewhat more normal in ladies yet in any case can show up in individuals of all ages who are passing on for any reason. The "final breath" happens somewhat in generally 50% of individuals who are dying.1

Individuals have needed to find out about death and kicking the bucket, and science has shown that it's a functioning interaction. There are steps in how the body closes down, similarly as there were ventures upon entering the world, during the youngster years, and in different phases of life. The final breath is one of those means and it

probably implies that demise is exceptionally close.

Is It Uncomfortable?
The final breath can be exceptionally hard so that relatives might be able to hear. In any case, a typical finish-of-life-altering situation isn't awkward for the people who are biting the dust, regardless of whether the individual appears to be somewhat conscious. It doesn't imply that the individual is "suffocating" or having a "terrible" death.2

Individuals who have a final breath while biting the dust experience no more difficulty breathing than the people who don't have one. Moreover, the nature of the final breath sounds you hear — how noisy they are, for instance — isn't a proportion of how much breathing misery there is. Indeed, even a portion of the medicines for a final breath will not be guaranteed to change the sounds.

Final breath sounds can be loud, however, they are not disturbing to the individual who is biting the dust.

As opposed to the perishing individual, nonetheless, the final breath can be extremely disturbing for friends and family, and parental figures. In one review, no less than 66% of friends and family of an individual kicking the bucket found that standing by listening to the final breath is exceptionally distressing.2

There are ways of evaporating a portion of the overabundant liquid that causes a final breath, however, recall that it is a normal move toward the withering system. Your cherished one doesn't feel like they are suffocating because they are breathing along these lines.

Is There a Treatment?
On the off chance that the final breath is making you restless, there are a couple of things you can attempt. They include:

Meds for liquid development: If you have a hospice solace pack, it probably has a prescription for evaporating the liquids. This is normally either atropine or scopolamine.3
Changing your cherished one's situation: The final breath might appear to be more terrible when somebody is lying level on their back. Turning your cherished ones over a piece might help. You can likewise have a go at setting the head higher than the body and going it aside to assist the liquids with depleting.

How Near Is Death?
Many individuals can't help thinking about how long it will be til' the very end when somebody fosters a final breath. It changes a

ton from one individual to another and makes it hard to foresee precisely the exact thing the clatter implies with regards to time.

You might consider what else to anticipate in the last phases of death. Terminal anxiety is normal as of now, and your cherished one might show up exceptionally fomented.

They likewise may communicate close demise mindfulness and let you know they are biting the dust. Many individuals right now talk about seeing friends and family who have kicked the bucket previously, and certain individuals even start to grin. Try not to attempt to address your adored one, simply love them.

Normal Symptoms toward the End of Life
Being Present
Being with your cherished one while they are kicking the bucket is testing, however, it is extremely adoring. At the point when

individuals discuss their biggest apprehension throughout everyday life, typically they will kick the bucket alone. Your presence is the best gift you can at any point give.

Try not to quit conversing with your cherished ones. Though hearing is the last sense to vanish, and regardless of whether they seem oblivious, they might in any case detect your presence or hear what you are saying.4

Simultaneously, you want to deal with yourself as your adored one would wish. Everybody needs a break sometimes, and this is a higher priority than at any other time. The fact that time is short makes the last breath only one sign. Make sure to take a second to stride away if you want to.

 Genuine Advice on How You Can Talk to a Dying Loved One
Rundown

The "final breath" is one sign that the end is very close, maybe surprisingly fast. It is exceptionally normal when somebody passes on. The murmuring sound is brought about by liquid that your adored one can never again hack up or swallow. It is difficult to hear, yet it is great to realize that it doesn't do any harm or damage your cherished one.

Here and there realizing a thing doesn't make it any simpler to encounter. That might be valid as you stand by listening to a friend or family member with a final breath, knowing in your mind that it's a typical piece of the perishing system yet feeling the pain in your heart. That is normal as well. Don't hesitate for even a moment to talk it over with a relative, the hospice group, or another person you trust to discuss these thoughts with.

Is murmuring equivalent to a final breath?

Murmuring most frequently depicts the sound of liquid in the lungs. It can happen as a component of the demise cycle. "Final breath" generally alludes to the commotion of spit pooling toward the rear of the throat.

Find out More: How to Identify and Treat Death Rattle/Wet Respirations
How might you tell a friend or family member who is close to death?
Cold skin, loud breathing, and loss of awareness are among the signs that demise might be close.

Not every person will display every one of them, yet it's great to realize them so you're ready to help your cherished one without showing dread or alert.
How long will an individual live once they foster a final breath?
Regularly, a final breath will start when an individual is hours from biting the dust, albeit certain individuals might keep on living for a little while.

Sirens sound for three minutes and afterward naturally switch off to safeguard their batteries. Assuming that they sound again that implies there is another peril, for example, a subsequent twister cautioning. Sirens are never sounded for an "all reasonable." You should pay attention to the radio or TV to see whether it is protected outside.

The outside cautioning sirens in Hennepin County will be actuated for twister admonitions, serious breezes at or surpassing 70 mph, or different circumstances when individuals ought to shield set up. At the point when the open-air cautioning sirens are enacted, they are just actuated in the areas/urban communities recorded in the advance notice polygon that is given by the National Weather Service.

Outdoor Warning Sirens exist to caution you to make a prompt life-saving move. Sirens are in many cases your LAST authority cautioning, coming just a brief time before a fierce tempest hits.

You ought to comprehend that Outdoor Warning Sirens caution individuals who are OUTSIDE that there is an impending risk. You should utilize alternate ways of getting advance notice when you are inside structures. A decent indoor ready framework is an NOAA Weather Radio.

At the point when you hear Outdoor Warning Sirens, it implies that you ought to: Sirens sound for extreme climate and other emergencies.NOAA
Maybe you heard the sirens cry in your neighborhood local area Wednesday around 1 p.m. The majority of us realize that is the month-to-month siren test directed by most Minnesota provinces and networks.

Yet, did you have at least some idea there are various strategies on when to blow the sirens in various networks around Minnesota?

For instance, a few Twin Cities-region provinces enact sirens for cyclone admonitions as well as tempests that produce 70 mph or extraordinary breezes. Here's data from the Ramsey County site.

For extreme climate, Ramsey County sirens are sounded for all cyclone admonitions and serious tempests with wind rates of at least 70 miles each hour.

Sirens sound for three minutes and afterward naturally switch off to safeguard their batteries. Assuming that they sound again that implies there is another peril, for example, a subsequent twister cautioning.

Sirens are never sounded for an "all reasonable." You should pay attention to the radio or TV to see whether it is protected outside.

The open-air cautioning sirens in Hennepin County will be actuated for cyclone alerts, extreme breezes at or surpassing 70 mph, or different circumstances when individuals ought to protect set up. At the point when the open-air cautioning sirens are actuated, they are just enacted in the areas/urban communities recorded in the advance notice polygon that is given by the National Weather Service.

You ought to comprehend that Outdoor Warning Sirens caution individuals who are OUTSIDE that there is an impending risk. You should utilize alternate ways of getting advance notice when you are inside structures. A decent indoor ready framework is an NOAA Weather Radio.
At the point when you hear Outdoor Warning Sirens, it implies that you ought to:

GET INSIDE implies finding a solid safe house right away. Go to the most minimal level. Track down a little room far away from outside windows. Get into a bath or other defensive spot like under a tough workbench. Safeguard your head with a protective cap if possible.

Common Emergency: The sign of a common crisis (like a cyclone) is a consistent cry heard for no less than 3 minutes

Keep in mind: Many sirens turn when they sound. Try not to befuddle expanding and diminishing volume with rising and falling tone.

Justifications for why Sirens are Not Mermaids - Siren versus Mermaid
are sirens, mermaids
Sirens are in many cases considered the dim and perilous forms of mermaids. In any case, are sirens mermaids? Or on the other hand, would they say they are various animals through and through? I examined them to figure out how comparable they truly are.

Today, sirens and mermaids are generally viewed as similar animals because their particular legends entwined over the last hundreds of years.

A few dialects like the sentiment dialects of Spanish and French and so on, don't for a moment even have separate terms for mermaids and sirens: They call the two mermaids and sirens sirenas (Spanish) and sirènes (French).

Yet, initially, sirens and mermaids were different animals in folklore. They didn't just appear to be unique yet in addition, acted totally in an unexpected way.

Chapter 3

Sirens lifestyle

In this article, I'll attempt to show you what the sirens were truly similar to and how various they were from mermaids. For this, we for the most part take a gander at the sirens and ocean fairies (who most mermaids depend on) from Greek folklore. Along these lines, how about we start.

1. Sirens are hazardous yet mermaids are well disposed
The greatest contrast between sirens and mermaids is the way that mermaids are by and large amicable animals while sirens are hazardous and even kill individuals.

In the most renowned story in which sirens showed up, the Odyssey, the legend Odysseus becomes cautioned about the sirens with the accompanying words:
"First you will raise the island of the Sirens, those animals who hypnotize any man alive, whoever comes in their direction.

Whoever draws excessively close, distracted, and gets the Sirens' voices in the air — no cruising home for him, no spouse ascending to meet him, no blissful youngsters radiating up at their dad's face. The high, exciting tune of the Sirens will captivate him, lolling there in their knoll, round them loads of cadavers decaying

endlessly, clothes of skin wilting on their bones."
That sounds pretty alarming. A few essayists later on even recommended that the sirens could have been barbarians, because of how

the last sentence portrays that the dead cadavers lay around them.

An elective translation would be that the people that made it alive to the island that the sirens lived on just starved to death since they were so mesmerized by the sirens that they didn't eat any longer.

How the sirens killed individuals was by baiting them near the rough island they lived on with the goal that the boats collided with the stones and soaked before their eyes.

The mermaids, then again, are agreeable, useful, and kind animals. The ocean sprites (nereids) represented the delightful and kind parts of the ocean and were addressed as extremely lovely young ladies.

They frequently wore parts of red coral as crowns were wearing white silk robes and in some cases rode on the rear of dolphins or hippocampi through the ocean. They moreover frequently saved mariners and anglers who were in peril on the ocean, at times, in any event, saving them from suffocating.

In this way, the mermaids are fundamentally something contrary to the sirens assuming you consider that sirens kill mariners and mermaids save them.

2. Sirens were initially bird ladies
Although Sirens are essentially consistently displayed as half lady half-fish figures like mermaids these days, they initially looked altogether different. In antiquated Greece, the sirens were considered half lady and half-bird animals.

The most seasoned portrayals in old Greek workmanship show them having large bird bodies with just a lady's head. They had bird feathers, which empowered them to fly, and paw-like bird feet.

Thus, first and foremost, they were something contrary to mermaids. Birds and fish have very little in like manner all things considered.

In the accompanying picture, you can see one of the most established portrayals of sirens in old Greece. It is a stamnos drawing from around 480-470 B.C. (Stamnos was a kind of old Greek stoneware that held fluids, like a jar.)

Since the sirens sing melodies that make each individual that hears them fall into a condition of daze and want to cruise towards them, they ordinarily indiscriminately collide with the rough bank of the sirens' island and bite the dust.

But since Odysseus was cautioned about this risk, he made his group stop up their ears with wax, so they couldn't hear the sirens.

Odysseus himself, be that as it may, was interested and chose to attach himself to the pole of his boat so he could hear the sirens' tune without flying off the handle and his life.

In the image, you can see Odysseus being attached to his pole while the sirens in the bird structure sing to him.

The portrayals in workmanship changed piece over time and in this manner, the presence of the sirens changed as well. Rather than being a bird with a lady's head, a piece later they were addressed as a lady with just the legs and wings of a bird (see point 3 for an image).

3. Sirens directed dead individuals to the otherworld
However, the sirens do not just kill individuals. They were additionally remembered to go with dead spirits from the human world to the otherworld.

Accordingly, they had a place with the psychopomps of Greek folklore: animals, spirits, and so forth who accompanied recently expired spirits from Earth to life following death. Thus, they were likewise frequently alluded to as the dreams of the lower world.

Because of this relationship as psychopomps, the old Greeks put siren sculptures on the graves of perished relatives. This was perceived as an emblematic portrayal of how their spirit was directed to the otherworld. In the image, you see such a sculpture.

The association with the otherworld probably came about because of their bird-like appearance or the alternate way around. Birds were now and again remembered to have the option to rise above the universes. This thought of dead birds that had an association with the domain of the spirits was fairly normal in some closeby societies around then [1].

In Syria figures of falcons on burial places likewise addressed the sides of the spirits and the old Egyptians even accepted that the spirit could leave a dead body as a bird (frequently a falcon).

Mermaids were anyway never connected with the dead or the otherworld. As depicted in point 1, they rather addressed the magnificence and life of the ocean.

4. Sirens just got their fishtails during the Middle Ages
In the wake of being portrayed as bird or half-lady and half-bird animals for a long time, in the middle age period, a few painters began giving the sirens fishtails as numerous mermaids had.

It appears to be that this adjustment of appearance was somewhat impacted by the freedoms the craftsmen took in introducing the sirens.

An Anglo-Latin inventory recorded and portrayed numerous beasts that were known during bygone eras. In the accompanying portion, you can peruse how the sirens were characterized in the book:

"Sirens are ocean young ladies, who bamboozle mariners with the remarkable magnificence of their appearance and the pleasantness of their tune, and are most similar to people from the head to the navel, with the body of a lady, yet have flaky fishes' tails, with which they generally sneak in the ocean."

A potential translation for the bird to fish change is that the wings of the sirens were excessively like the wings of the heavenly messengers and consequently their appearance wasn't as per the thoughts of Christianity and must be changed [2].

Perhaps the way that the sirens' folks were ocean divine beings (see point 7) and the sirens killed mariners in the ocean additionally affected the choice to portray them with fish-tails rather than bird parts.

By and large, it isn't excessively business as usual that their portrayals changed. All things considered, in antiquated texts like the Odyssey, the sirens' appearance was not determined.

However, the mermaids never went through such a sensational change. The Tritons generally had a fishtail. Simply the nereids were for the most part portrayed in human structure and just at times with tails.

Yet, by and large, fishtails were related to the mermen (Tritons) and their female renditions for quite a while. There were even a couple of new water sprites and divine beings (for example Achilles) with fishtails.

5. Sirens were portrayed with wings and two tails however mermaids were not
As referenced the wings of the sirens were generally a leftover of their bird days (and their psychopomp character) and were utilized in portrayals for some additional time.

Although the sirens were presently portrayed with a mermaid tail, they had most qualities that the sirens from the old Greek fantasies likewise had: in particular their perilous nature and ability to draw mariners to their demise with their voice.

Simply how they were deciphered had changed during the standard of Christianity.

This better approach for deciphering the sirens as evil ladies that tempt men is believed to be the justification for why sirens were likewise portrayed with two tails on many temples and structures in Europe during the hour of the late Middle Ages: as a disconcerting portrayal of corruption

The word siren comes from the old Greek word seirḗn (Σειρήν). The historical underpinnings of that word aren't completely clear + it is by all accounts got from the Semitic root for singing.

Others proposed that the word may be associated with the Greek word for "rope, the string" (σειρά = seirá), which would allude to how they tie individuals through their charming voice or even to how Odysseus must be bound to the pole of his boat to endure them.

The word mermaid then again is of Old English beginning and signifies "a little kid from the ocean" from simple (ocean) and servant (young lady or young lady).

And, surprisingly, the Greek words for the ocean sprites mirrored areas of strength for this ocean. The nereids are fundamentally called "the wet/watery ones" because their name is gotten from their dad Nereus and his name is thusly gotten from the old Greek word "neros" signifying "water".

The base of the name of the Tritonides which comes from their dad Triton isn't precisely clear, yet it appears to have an association with a Celtic word that signifies "ocean" (triath, declined trethan).

As may be obvious, the word siren is firmly attached to their perilous voice while the words for mermaid mirror major areas of strength for them to the water and the ocean.

7. In Greek folklore sirens and mermaids had various roots
At the point when you take a gander at the genealogy of the Greek divine beings, sprites, and beasts, you can see that sirens and mermaids were quite far away from one another.

In the accompanying infographic that I made, you can see that the sirens were essential for the time of the early stage divine beings on the highest point of the tree while the mermaids (ocean fairies and Tritonides) were important for the period of the Olympian divine beings on the actual lower part of the genealogy.

mermaid versus siren genealogy of greek folklore on which you can see that they are far separated
Siren versus Mermaid genealogical record in Greek folklore.
The sirens were the little girls of the ocean god Phorcys and the ocean goddess Ceto. The intriguing thing is that their youngsters were all ocean beasts!

Other than the sirens, their youngsters included Scylla (ocean beast with a few canine heads), the Gorgons (Medusa and her two sisters who had snakes as hair and could transform everybody into stone), and the Graeae (3 witches who just had one eye and tooth which they alternated utilizing).

This proposes that the sirens ought to be delegated beasts also. It ought to anyway be referenced, that in a few later texts a couple of explicit sirens were depicted as the girls of the stream god (Potamoi) Achilles.

However, I chose to adhere to the more established sources that characterized them as the girls of Phorcys and Ceto. For an incredible outline of the genealogy of Greek folklore, look at this video by UsefulCharts on Youtube.

The mermaids, then again, that is the ocean fairies like the nereids and Tritonides, are the little girls of ocean divine beings and water or ocean sprites. So their well-disposed nature and magnificence were in a real sense in their qualities because of their fairy moms.

8. There were a couple of sirens however a lot more mermaids

As indicated by Homer, who composed the Odyssey, there were just two sirens. Other Greek writers anyway guaranteed that there were somewhere in the range of three and eight.

They were now and again given names too, yet these differed from one artist to another. An illustration of the names they were given is the names Peisinoe, Aglaope, and Thelxiepeia.

The mermaids were undeniably more in number in Greek folklore. There were precisely 50 nereids of which some additionally had youngsters.

The quantity of the Tritonides wasn't expressed, however since mermaids, as opposed to the sirens, are known to duplicate, almost certainly, they have increased throughout the long term. This truly intends that there would be at least thousands of mermaids at this point.

9. Sirens initially lived on a rough island yet mermaids lived in the sea
As referenced previously, as per the old Greek legends, particularly the account of Odysseus, the sirens lived on an island that was encircled by precipices and rocks.

Such rough beaches are one of the most perilous spots for boats to pass since they can undoubtedly get found out in the wild flows and crush against the stones which can make them sink.
Given how hazardous the waves can become in such places the mariners would frequently bite the dust, regardless of whether they got transported on time.

This association with a risky way of water, that must be passed, was a basic piece of the tales about the sirens.

They were straightforwardly connected to the perilous coastline, or perhaps they were a portrayal of them, very much like numerous animals in Greek folklore addressed and refined a piece of nature.

In such a manner, the sirens appear to be like the two other ocean beasts from the Odyssey: Charybdis and Scylla. You can peruse more about the marine danger the sirens are associated with and the genuine islands they lived on in my post about whether sirens are genuine.

As referenced in point 7, Scylla was a sister of the sirens. In this way, the association between the risky rough coastline before that island that the sirens lived on and the sirens' approach to tricking in and killing mariners appears to have a comparable root. Mermaid versus siren areas as indicated by Greek folklore.

Mermaids, then again, were dependably ocean inhabitants and not bound to a particular island or region.

The Nereids were said to reside in the Aegean Sea among Greece and Turkey, where they remained in a brilliant castle in the profundities with their dad Nereus (near where the mermaid is in the image).

However, the other ocean fairies, the offspring of Triton, really experienced all around the Mediterranean Sea. Also, when the god Triton ventured to every part of the ocean, both the Nereids and Tritons frequently followed him.

So you could say that they were home in the entirety of the Mediterranean Sea.

10. Sirens just showed up in Greek folklore however mermaids do in fantasies from around the world
The sirens are Greek ocean animals.

Even though there were a couple of comparable bird animals in different societies and, surprisingly, in Greek folklore itself there were the shrews, they didn't have a similar story as the sirens, who tricked mariners to their demise. The wenches, for instance, just took food and bothered certain individuals.

There are anyway two legends that look similar to how the sirens baited mariners. Right off the bat, there is a Danish and Swedish middle-age melody wherein mythical people attempt to entice men with their lovely singing.

Besides, there is the narrative of the Loreley, a mermaid that lives at the riskiest way of the Rhine stream and baits mariners to their demise by singing. In any case, this story is based on a sonnet by the German creator Clemens Brentano, which he wrote in 1801.

So both of these accounts were perhaps affected by the sirens from Greek folklore (the Loreley certainly), whose story was recorded by Homer as soon as around 675-725 B.C. Furthermore, consequently, you can express that there isn't exactly a comparable fantasy out there.

Mermaids do anyway have partners all over the planet. The earliest legend about a mermaid comes from Syria. quite a while back Atargatis lost her significant other and attempted to overwhelm herself with bitterness.

Yet, the powers of the water changed her into a mermaid and let her live on. She was revered as a fruitful goddess around there and all around the Mediterranean for quite a while.

Different mermaids are the Mami Water from Africa, the Nixies from Germany and

Scandinavia, the Yawkyawk from Australia, and some more.

11. Sirens are just female however mermaids have male partners
In the old Greek texts, sirens were just at any point depicted as female. Perhaps because it is simpler for females to bait in the male mariners with their voices.

In imaginative depictions, you could consider male sirens to be well, yet just for an exceptionally brief time frame until around the fifth century BC.
Whenever they were portrayed as part lady and bird or fish they were consistently female in workmanship as well, very much like in the legends. During the hundreds of years, particularly in Christian conviction during the archaic time, they came to address the hazardous female enticement that could deceive men.

Thus, any reasonable person would agree that sirens were only female animals.

Mermaids, then again, had a ton of male partners before and today. The most popular merman is unquestionably Triton. He was for the most part portrayed with a fishtail

Triton was the sort of the ocean and his kids (or his purification) were known as the Tritons (guys) and Tritonides (females). The Tritons were Poseidon's partners (other than certain Nereids) who generally went with him on his movements through the ocean.

Very much like Triton they had fishtails. To flag that Poseidon was coming, they were blowing
their conch shells.

a Tritone merman sculpture with a hippocampus on the trevi wellspring

A fish-followed Tritone (one of Triton's children) with a Hippocampus on the Trevi Fountain in Rome.

Besides, the nereids likewise had one sibling called Nerites.

12. Sirens don't experience passionate feelings for men, just mermaids do

Despite the fact that sirens are frequently connected with the emblematic enticement of men, they entirely were keen on men in a heartfelt manner.

In none of the first legends, they showed any interest in them, aside from when it came to killing them. Mermaids, then again, were for the most part keen on men. This is on the grounds that fairies overall frequently had a specific interest in people.

For instance, in the Odyssey, Odysseus was held hostage by a fairy called Calypso (an ocean sprite as per a few essayists) for quite a long time since she became hopelessly enamored with him and needed to make him her eternal spouse.

A portion of the ocean fairies even got hitched, similar to the two most notable nereids, Amphitrite and Thetys. Amphitrite was the spouse of the ocean god Poseidon (and mother of Triton) and Thetis was even hitched to a human man, the legend Peleus. Be that as it may, Thetis was constrained into the marriage and was not in adoration with her significant other.

The mermaids' propensity to go gaga for men was most prominently expounded on in the writing of the heartfelt period with the tale of the Little Mermaid by Hans Christian Andersen from 1837 and its Disney transformation about Ariel being the most compelling one.

13. Sirens didn't have an association with the ocean like mermaids did

Mermaids or ocean sprites were essential for the ocean and experienced all around the Mediterranean. Like different sprites from Greek folklore, which are all nature spirits, they had major areas of strength for nature and the component that they lived in.

For instance, the new water fairies like the Oceanids and Naiads were the human types of the streams, streams, springs, and so on they each addressed and really focused on.

Additionally, different fairies, similar to tree sprites, addressed their trees over which they watched.

After the legend Perseus killed the beast Medusa, which had the ability to turn everybody that took a gander at her to stone, he perceived how Andromeda, the little girl of the lord of Aethiopia, was compromised by an ocean beast and rushed to her salvage. The top of the dead Medusa was still in his sack and before he protected the young lady, he put Medusa's head on some ocean growth on the edge of the water.

There something amazing occurred. The blood of Medusa trickled into the ocean growth and transformed it into what resembled red stone - coral!
The ocean sprites saw this and were entranced to such an extent that they immediately accumulated more green growth, absorbed in the blood, and afterward established the recently developed corals on the ocean bed. Thus, as per this legend, the mermaids were liable for spreading the corals in the Mediterranean Sea.

Other than that, they additionally were said to have specific abilities that were associated with the ocean.
Sirens did not have such an association with nature and the ocean. This is most likely because of the way that they lived on their island and not in the actual ocean and that

they were occupied with tricking mariners to their demise.

14. Sirens could spellbind people with their voice, yet mermaids didn't

The sirens' entrancing voices were one of the greatest contrasts with mermaids. The sirens were characterized by the way that they tricked mariners to their demise by singing their captivating and powerful tunes to them.

The accompanying artwork portrays clearly the way that hypnotized Odysseus looks bound to his pole when he experiences the singing sirens.

Their tunes are otherwise called siren melodies today and address the captivating and spellbinding magnificence of their singing.

Mermaids, then again, were initially not as emphatically connected with melody and

music, particularly not with mesmerizing people.
Today their wonderful voices are an essential piece of their being also, as you

can find in motion pictures like Ariel, the Little Mermaid, and others.
In any case, this affiliation, that mermaids are melodic, really came from the sirens when the two ideas of the mermaid and siren began to converge during the Middle Ages. The musicality was never a characterizing element of the ocean sprites and mermaids before that.

15. Sirens were many times portrayed playing instruments yet mermaids were not
As referenced previously, from the start, the sirens were portrayed as birds with ladies' heads. Birds are constantly connected with delightful melodies.

Yet, when craftsmen began to attract them to a greater extent a human structure, whether as half-bird or half-fish, they required something that showed their musicality from the get-go

and their new human arms were wonderful to hold instruments.
The ocean sprites were anyway never portrayed or depicted with an instrument. The main to some degree melodic thing they did was the point at which the Tritons blew their conch shells to flag that Poseidon was on his way over the ocean.

16. Sirens were managers of insight and taboo information
The tunes that the sirens sang were delightful songs, however, they really made vows to confess to give their casualties secret information or educate them something regarding themselves which made their melodies significantly seriously captivating.

A few researchers even portrayed them as mantic animals that knew both the past and what was in store You can grasp the reason why on the off chance that

you view what they share with Odysseus in the Odyssey:
"When he hears however much he might want, sails on, a savvier man. We know every one of the torments that the Greeks and Trojans once persevered on the spreading plain of Troy when the divine beings willed it so —all that happens on the prolific earth, we know everything!"

They offer to let him know something that will bring him illumination, and make him a smarter man.Anyway, this is a bogus commitment, as they probably won't let him know this mysterious information Afterall and on second thought kill him.
Mermaids then again, don't have such an endowment of information.

17. Sirens kicked the bucket in unexpected ways in comparison to mermaids did

As per a few post-Homeric creators, the sirens just needed to kick the bucket, on the off chance that somebody heard regardless of their entrancing singing. This would imply that they would have passed on after Odysseus heard them.

In any case, others say that they are essentially undying, particularly since they were many times portrayed as the partners of the god Hades from the otherworld.

Mermaids, as sprites, were likewise extremely enduring.

It isn't exceptionally clear on the off chance that they passed on, yet since most sprites bite the dust when the piece of nature they address kicks the bucket (like a tree, waterway, and so on) it appears to be logical that the ocean fairies just passed on the off chance that the ocean they live in evaporated or perhaps were very contaminated so the existence inside was unimaginable any longer.